FRANCIS FRITH'S

MERSEYSIDE

LIVING MEMORIES

Although born in the south, **Derryck Draper** has lived in northern England for over thirty years, and for the last ten of those in Southport. He is a founder member of the Outdoors Writers Guild, and has written for many outdoor activity magazines. He is currently editor of an international performance textiles publication.

FRANCIS FRITH'S
PHOTOGRAPHIC MEMORIES

MERSEYSIDE
LIVING MEMORIES

DERRYCK DRAPER

First published in paperback in the United Kingdom in 2004 by
Frith Book Company Ltd

Paperback Edition 2004
ISBN 1-85937-673-8

British Library Cataloguing in Publication Data

Francis Frith's Merseyside Living Memories
Derryck Draper

Frith Book Company Ltd
Frith's Barn, Teffont,
Salisbury, Wiltshire SP3 5QP
Tel: +44 (0) 1722 716 376
Email: info@francisfrith.co.uk
www.francisfrith.co.uk

Printed and bound in Great Britain

Front Cover: **LIVERPOOL,** *Ranelagh Street* *c1950* L60033
Frontispiece: **NEW BRIGHTON,** *The Front c1960* N14033

*The colour-tinting is for illustrative purposes only, and is not intended to be
historically accurate*

AS WITH ANY HISTORICAL DATABASE THE FRITH ARCHIVE IS CONSTANTLY
BEING CORRECTED AND IMPROVED, AND THE PUBLISHERS WOULD
WELCOME INFORMATION ON OMISSIONS OR INACCURACIES

CONTENTS

FRANCIS FRITH
VICTORIAN PIONEER

FRANCIS FRITH, founder of the world-famous photographic archive, was a complex and multi-talented man. A devout Quaker and a highly successful Victorian businessman, he was philosophical by nature and pioneering in outlook.

By 1855 he had already established a wholesale grocery business in Liverpool, and sold it for the astonishing sum of £200,000, which is the equivalent today of over £15,000,000. Now a very rich man, he was able to indulge his passion for travel. As a child he had pored over travel books written by early explorers, and his fancy and imagination had been stirred by family holidays to the sublime mountain regions of Wales and Scotland. 'What lands of spirit-stirring and enriching scenes and places!' he had written. He was to return to these scenes of grandeur in later years to 'recapture the thousands of vivid and tender memorles', but with a different purpose. Now in his thirties, and captivated by the new science of photography, Frith set out on a series of pioneering journeys up the Nile and to the Near East that occupied him from 1856 unti 1860.

INTRIGUE AND EXPLORATION

These far-flung journeys were packed with intrigue and adventure. In his life story, written when he was sixty-three, Frith tells of being held captive by bandits, and of fighting 'an awful midnight battle to the very point of surrender with a deadly pack of hungry, wild dogs'. Wearing flowing Arab costume, Frith arrived at Akaba by camel sixty years before Lawrence of Arabia, where he encountered 'desert princes and rival sheikhs, blazing with jewel-hilted swords'.

He was the first photographer to venture beyond the sixth cataract of the Nile. Africa was still the mysterious 'Dark Continent', and Stanley and Livingstone's historic meeting was a decade into the future. The conditions for picture taking confound belief. He laboured for hours in his wicker dark-room in the sweltering heat of the desert, while the volatile chemicals fizzed dangerously in their trays. Back in London he exhibited his photographs and was 'rapturously cheered' by members of the Royal Society. His reputation as a photographer was made overnight.

VENTURE OF A LIFE-TIME

Characteristically, Frith quickly spotted the opportunity to create a new business as a specialist publisher of photographs. He lived in an era of immense and sometimes violent change. For the poor in the early part of Victoria's reign work was exhausting and the hours long, and people had precious little free time to enjoy themselves. Most people had no transport other than a cart or gig at their disposal, and rarely

business one only has to look at the catalogue issued by Frith & Co in 1886: it runs to some 670 pages, listing not only many thousands of views of the British Isles but also many photographs of most European countries, and China, Japan, the USA and Canada - note the sample page shown on page 9 from the hand-written Frith & Co ledgers recording the pictures. By 1890 Frith had created the greatest specialist photographic publishing company in the world, with over 2,000 sales outlets - more than the combined number that Boots and WH Smith have today! The picture on the next page shows the Frith & Co display board at Ingleton in the Yorkshire Dales (left of window). Beautifully constructed with a mahogany frame and gilt inserts, it could display up to a dozen local scenes.

travelled far beyond the boundaries of their own town or village. However, by the 1870s the railways had threaded their way across the country, and Bank Holidays and half-day Saturdays had been made obligatory by Act of Parliament. All of a sudden the working man and his family were able to enjoy days out and see a little more of the world.

With typical business acumen, Francis Frith foresaw that these new tourists would enjoy having souvenirs to commemorate their days out. In 1860 he married Mary Ann Rosling and set out on a new career: his aim was to photograph every city, town and village in Britain. For the next thirty years he travelled the country by train and by pony and trap, producing fine photographs of seaside resorts and beauty spots that were keenly bought by millions of Victorians. These prints were painstakingly pasted into family albums and pored over during the dark nights of winter, rekindling precious memories of summer excursions.

THE RISE OF FRITH & CO

Frith's studio was soon supplying retail shops all over the country. To meet the demand he gathered about him a small team of photographers, and published the work of independent artist-photographers of the calibre of Roger Fenton and Francis Bedford. In order to gain some understanding of the scale of Frith's

POSTCARD BONANZA

The ever-popular holiday postcard we know today took many years to develop. In 1870 the Post Office issued the first plain cards, with a pre-printed stamp on one face. In 1894 they allowed other publishers' cards to be sent through the mail with an attached adhesive halfpenny stamp. Demand grew rapidly, and in 1895 a new size of postcard was permitted called the court card, but there was little room for illustration. In 1899, a year after Frith's death, a new card measuring 5.5 x 3.5 inches became the standard format, but it was not until 1902 that the divided back came into being, so that the address and message could be on one face and a full-size illustration on the other. Frith & Co were in the vanguard of postcard development: Frith's sons Eustace and Cyril continued their father's monumental task, expanding the number of views offered to the public and recording more and more places in Britain, as the coasts and countryside were opened up to mass travel.

Francis Frith had died in 1898 at his villa in Cannes, his great project still growing. The archive he created continued in business for another seventy years. By 1970 it contained over a third of a million pictures showing 7,000 British towns and villages.

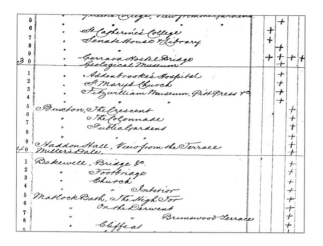

FRANCIS FRITH'S LEGACY

Frith's legacy to us today is of immense significance and value, for the magnificent archive of evocative photographs he created provides a unique record of change in the cities, towns and villages throughout Britain over a century and more. Frith and his fellow studio photographers revisited locations many times down the years to update their views, compiling for us an enthralling and colourful pageant of British life and character.

We are fortunate that Frith was dedicated to recording the minutiae of everyday life. For it is this sheer wealth of visual data, the painstaking chronicle of changes in dress, transport, street layouts, buildings, housing, engineering and landscape that captivates us so much today. His remarkable images offer us a powerful link with the past and with the lives of our ancestors.

THE VALUE OF THE ARCHIVE TODAY

Computers have now made it possible for Frith's many thousands of images to be accessed almost instantly. Frith's images are increasingly used as visual resources, by social historians, by researchers into genealogy and ancestry, by architects and town planners, and by teachers involved in local history projects.

In addition, the archive offers every one of us an opportunity to examine the places where we and our families have lived and worked down the years. Highly successful in Frith's own era, the archive is now, a century and more on, entering a new phase of popularity. Historians consider the Francis Frith Collection to be of prime national importance. It is the only archive of its kind remaining in private ownership. Francis Frith's archive is now housed in an historic timber barn in the beautiful village of Teffont in Wiltshire. Its founder would not recognize the archive office as it is today. In place of the many thousands of dusty boxes containing glass plate negatives and an all-pervading odour of photographic chemicals, there are now ranks of computer screens. He would be amazed to watch his images travelling round the world at unimaginable speeds through internet lines.

The archive's future is both bright and exciting. Francis Frith, with his unshakeable belief in making photographs available to the greatest number of people, would undoubtedly approve of what is being done today with his lifetime's work. His photographs depicting our shared past are now bringing pleasure and enlightenment to millions around the world a century and more after his death.

MERSEYSIDE
AN INTRODUCTION

MERSEYSIDE - A PLACE FOR ALL REASONS

WHEN asked to write this book I had to consider whether the subject was to be Merseyside as in 'strictly on the banks of the River Mersey', or as in the shambles of political expediency that was the result of the 1974 boundary changes. The latter example of greed and naked ambition ignored the history and geographical logic of so much of our great country, and in particular of the northern counties - the true powerhouse of Britain, whether Whitehall likes it or no.

Because of the wanderings by Frith photographers of the past, my result is something of a compromise, but it acknowledges, I hope, the input of many, many generations into that part of Britain where two great old counties meet and use a mighty river to cement the join. Both Cheshire and Lancashire have served our monarchy and country well; the River Mersey has provided a thoroughfare carrying goods and people to the base of the Pennine Hills. Together they are Merseyside.

NEW BRIGHTON, *The Fort c1960* N14013

For ages past, this strip of the English coastline between the Rivers Dee and Ribble has been salt marsh and wind-piled sand dunes. Its shallow beaches are deceptively quiescent, but its reputation for danger requires pilots and masters to take care when sailing into the Irish Sea. Broken-backed ships are just as likely without the existence of rocks on which to impale them, and there are more than a few hulls lying in the shallow seas off Liverpool Bay.

Whilst the area was undoubtedly thinly populated before the 10th century, it was the arrival of the Norsemen - the Vikings - from Dublin and Man that brought settlement and land conversion to a part of Britain that had hitherto promised nothing except thin pickings and a subsistence-level existence at best. It has always been a matter of some ironic amusement that it was the descendents of the Vikings' Irish landlords - who had thrown them out of the Emerald Isle - that later came looking for a helping hand when times became hard nearly eight hundred years later.

The Scandinavian legacy is two-fold. We see it first in the place names: those ending in -by or -ton indicate a settlement, and are usually preceded by the family name; others indicate the use of a place – for instance, Thingwall means the meeting place of the elders on the Wirral. Secondly, it is thanks to the Vikings that the land is productive (with the exception of a narrow strip within sight of the sea), and is capable of sustaining crops and animals - we can survive without strawberries at Christmas, no matter what the supermarkets tell us!

Having previously made a few fleeting visits to Merseyside, a decade or so ago I made the area my home and have come to appreciate the value to be gained from visiting places where most of the history is still on the surface. The ethnic mix is as eclectic as one should expect from close proximity to what was once one of the world's major ports. Mention the name Liverpool in any country and it is instantly recognised, with about a 60/40 split in linking the city with the Beatles and its soccer clubs. The humour is good, and mostly non-injurious. There are areas of social injustice and some deprivation, but no worse than any other part of the United Kingdom.

CITY AND HEART

Liverpool, and its position at the gateway to the Atlantic, is the regional pivot on which almost everything has swung for the past three hundred and fifty years. It is no exaggeration to say that the grand buildings which grace much of the Liverpool skyline and waterfront are founded on the financial gains from slavery. The city's entrepreneurs saw an opportunity in slave trading in 1700 and embraced it wholeheartedly. It prospered on the operation of the system know as 'triangular trading': cotton textiles and manufactured goods were sent to West Africa, to be exchanged for slaves, who were in turn taken to the southern states of America and the West Indies to be exchanged again for sugar, alcohol, tobacco and raw cotton.

After slavery was abolished during the first decade of the 1800s, the port took on a different character as it shipped emigrant hopefuls from northern Europe to the USA and the Antipodes. The figure of some nine million people has been given as the size of this particular aspect of 'exporting'. By the same token - although in nothing like the same numbers - a considerable number of immigrants from a wide diversity of nationalities made their homes in Liverpool during the same period, roughly 1830 to 1930.

The vigour of the Irishness of the city is very apparent even more than a century after the Irish potato famine, and the world's first Chinatown still maintains modern values with losing any of its inscrutability and without compromising the strength of the familial system.

In 2008 Liverpool will be the European Capital of Culture, and the city has experienced a resurgence of pride that surprised many detractors of the appointment. Comparisons are being reasonably drawn with Manchester as the spending power of the port edges upwards to meet that of its rival in the north west.

CHINA CUPS, LACE CURTAINS AND CATS

The Wirral has always seen itself as Cheshire, and no amount of government tinkering and gerrymandering will ever change that conviction.

The residents of the eastern towns may find that they are geographically closer to Liverpool and may perhaps earn their daily crust in the city, but they are unlikely to even vaguely consider themselves as Scousers, despite a similar accent.

Birkenhead and Wallasey docks developed because the waters were deeper than on the opposite bank of the Mersey and so the bulk carriers found it easier to dock there. The hills of Wirral provided protection from the prevailing westerlies and there was plenty of room for expansion. The Great Float dock provided employment directly and indirectly for over a hundred years before competition from Europe and improvements in road transport sent it into decline.

Following several plots and plans, the land at the eastern end of the Great Float has been

THORNTON HOUGH, *The Entrance to Thornton Manor c1950* T221005

developed as the Twelve Quays. It facilitates a ferry service between Merseyside and Ireland that has moved from the Liverpool side of the river: the ferries can save an hour on an Irish Sea crossing because they no longer have to travel through Liverpool's enclosed dock system. There is also a new floating stage that can handle two roll-on/roll-off ferries simultaneously.

Wallasey and Bidston Docks have been filled. Morpeth and Egerton Docks have been improved environmentally, and their quaysides have been developed for use by light industry and administration services. They have also echoed the developments at the Albert Dock in Liverpool in providing a home for museums and galleries.

West Wirral provides as big a contrast as it's possible to find. With not even an echo of the commercial activity on the other side of the peninsular, this is the dormitory for the middle classes and a haven for those seeking quieter pleasures. Leading industrialists made - and continue to make - their homes there, and the number of large estates has changed but little.

In 2006 the Open golf championship will be hosted by the Royal Liverpool Golf Club at its Hoylake base for the first time since 1967. In the intervening years the demands of the Open in terms of infrastructure, space and traffic management have ruled out the club as an appropriate venue. Now, however, with plans in place as a result of the three-way agreement signed by the Royal and Ancient Golf Club, Royal Liverpool Golf Club and the Metropolitan Borough of Wirral, the Open will make a welcome and long-overdue return after a break of 39 years.

Some of the pictures on the following pages show the views across the Dee estuary to the Welsh hills. When viewing those, it should be borne in mind that commercial fishing was the one industry carried out from these quiet shores. Almost defunct now, there are nevertheless a few pockets of stubborn resistance by part-time inshore fisherman as they supplement their income in a traditional manner.

In my estimation The Wirral as a whole changes but slowly. It is a land of good manners and tea time, of lace curtains and the grins of disappearing cats.

HAPPENSTANCE

Southport owes its existence to one man's endeavours in providing a bathing shelter on the North Meols shore. A poor thing of shipwreck timbers and rough thatch, it nevertheless was the first building in what was called initially New Marsh and later Lord Street. The Duke's Folly was the second building, a lodging house erected beside the bathing shelter; it took its title from William Sutton's nickname, a comment on his preoccupation with European royalty. The town grew as a form of health resort in the early 1800s, and was often quoted as enjoying mild airs and a temperate climate at all times of the year.

Modern Southport plays a leading part in the prosperity of the Metropolitan Borough of Sefton; its hotels, clubs and seaside attractions bring many thousands to the area. Recent developments have all been angled towards the capture of more of the leisure market, with the annual garden show, the air show and the fireworks competition all serving to bring potential customers within the orbit of the town's entrepreneurs. Lord Street is famed as a striking example of a Victorian boulevard-style shopping centre. Its glazed canopies are built over ground that was originally the front gardens of the buildings fronting the thoroughfare.

Birkdale and Ainsdale to the immediate south have stature as highly desirable residential areas. Although now part of Southport, they had their origins in townships much older than their present-day sponsor. Both enjoy an uncluttered foreshore and some of the finest golf links in England.

NORTHERN GRIT

In contrast with the open views of the coastline towns, St Helens, Eaglestown and Newton-le-Willows owe their form and structure to the Industrial Revolution. Coal mining, glass production, chemical plants and foundries - plus the necessary means of transport for the finished products - brought prosperity to the area from the middle of the 18th century through to the middle of the 20th. However, in common with so much of Britain's industrial capacity, a steady decline since the 1960s has vastly reduced the working environment. Glass manufacturing and develop-

ment still remains the largest employer in the area, but pretty well all else has closed down.

Service industries are filling the gap, and improved transport links have given young people the opportunity to work in the cities of Liverpool and Manchester. Nearby Warrington has also developed a strong local economy, with a corresponding labour requirement that is not entirely met by the local workforce.

These communities are situated in countryside that retains its beauty despite the industrial past. The Sankey Canal, logged as the first canal of the Industrial Revolution, was closed in 1963 after the sugar trade between Liverpool and Earlestown ended in 1959. In recent years a restoration group has achieved much success in persuading the local authority to cooperate in an extensive programme of renovation, with the intention using the waterway as a leisure facility and living museum.

ST HELENS, *Church Street c1965* S415040

THE WIRRAL

NEW BRIGHTON
The Lighthouse c1960
N14004

Constructed from granite blocks cemented together with 'puzzellani', a special hardening material developed from volcanic dust extracted from the slopes of Mount Etna, the lighthouse was inaugurated in March 1830; it replaced an original wooden structure dating back to 1683. In the late 1980s it was sold, refurbished and subsequently marketed as a quirky site for honeymooners and those enjoying esoteric weekend breaks.

NEW BRIGHTON
The Fort c1960 N14013

Built in the late1820s, Fort Perch Rock Battery site was then manned continuously until the end of World War II. On what is evidently a cool day, the visitors of the 1960s are nevertheless enjoying the traditions of a day by the sea - a trip round the bay and a bracing stroll to the lighthouse.

NEW BRIGHTON, *The Marine Promenade c1960* N14033

Local records show that the Melody Inn Revue (note the poster, right) ran continuously at the Floral Pavilion from 1948 until 1970. Stacked trays and a couple of van men (centre left) suggest that Scott's bakery (no longer in operation) is making its daily delivery to the Pavilion tea rooms.

NEW BRIGHTON, *The Beach and the Pier c1960* N14024

All the elements of a successful British seaside holiday in the middle of the 20th century are here - deckchairs, donkey rides and a selection of pedalos for hire. The traditional pier is an endangered species in modern Britain, and this particular example only lasted for another decade. In 1962 a combination of a high tide and gales so damaged the passenger walkways at the end of the structure that the ferry service to Liverpool was discontinued.

DETAIL FROM N14024

NEW BRIGHTON
the Pier c1960 N14038

NEW BRIGHTON, *The Pier c1960* N14039

Notice the almost formal clothing of the seaside visitors – the women all wearing dresses or skirts, children in smart footwear and ankle socks, and the men clad in jackets, pullovers and ties! In the 21st century the option of a toffee apple being 'made before your eyes' (as the stall centre right boasts) without an EU directive is something at which one can only wonder.

NEW BRIGHTON
The Tower c1960 N14037

Seen across the boating lake, the Tower buildings rise impressively as the centrepiece of New Brighton's attractions. The original tower was built in 1898 to a height of 621 feet, but neglect during World War I rendered the upper structure unsafe, and it was dismantled at the beginning of the 1920s. In the background are the ferris wheel and the aerial cars of the popular fairgrounds. The Tower buildings were finally demolished after an extensive fire in 1969.

NEW BRIGHTON, *The Bathing Pool c1950* N14311

Opened in 1934, the bathing pool was one of the largest in the world and capable of holding 4,000 swimmers and 20,000 spectators. This made it the ideal venue for the annual Miss New Brighton competition, which was first held in 1949 and continued for the next 40years. The complex was demolished in 1991 after being severely damaged by gales during the previous winter.

LEASOWE
The Castle c1965 L233010

Built in 1592 for Ferdinand, 5th Earl of Derby, to enable him to watch horse-racing on the sands at Meols, Leasowe Castle was converted into a hotel in 1982. The original entrance and coat of arms, a mounting stone for horsemen and the winding staircase to the old tower are still intact. The fact that it overlooks Leasowe Golf Course is an added attraction for patrons.

WALLASEY, *The Village c1955*
W164005

Linking Harrison Drive and Breck Road, Wallasey Village has always been just that; no Road, Drive, Way or other title, because it doesn't need it. The scene in the photograph bears little resemblance to the same street today, although many of the buildings are still visible. An onslaught of traffic-controlling measures made necessary by the proximity of the entrance to the Kingsway Tunnel under the River Mersey has made parking at the kerbside an art form seldom seen now. The tradesman in the Reliant Regent three-wheeled van (left) would be risking a screen full of parking tickets in modern Wallasey.

WALLASEY
Leasowe Road c1960
W164022

As an approach to Junction 1 of the M53 motorway, Leasowe Road (A551) is now dual carriageway for much of its length. The semi-rural urbanity in this photograph has given way to fast-food outlets and the steady rumble of passing traffic. The vehicle at the kerb on the left belongs to Heavysege Limited, a local wine, spirit and beer wholesaler noted for its bottling of Younger's bitter.

WALLASEY
St Hilary's Church
c1955 W164014

Situated at the landward end of Wallasey Village and built in 1859, the present parish church of St Hilary replaced an earlier 16th-century building destroyed by fire in 1857. Many of the building's stained glass windows were damaged in World War II, and a new east window was installed in 1955.

WALLASEY, *Chalets off Harrison Drive c1965* W164068

Seaside chalets have formed an integral part of British seaside holidays for well over a hundred years. Nowadays a great many are privately owned, and occasionally change hands for considerable sums. Those pictured back on to what is now a miniature golf course and car park.

WALLASEY
*Harrison Drive
Beach c1965*
W164059

WALLASEY, *Dinghy sailing from Harrison Drive Beach c1965* W164073

Long shadows indicate the end of a pleasurable day's sailing from this well-known beach. The resorts of the Wirral are well known for their long association with small craft usage and sail training.

BIRKENHEAD, *The Docks c1965* B399085

BIRKENHEAD
The Docks c1965
B399087

BIRKENHEAD
The Docks c1965 B399091

By 1965 the docks at Birkenhead were in severe decline, as we can see from the sparse shipping in these views. The flour mills (B399087, left background) are a reminder of the port's heyday when the trading vessels of the world would have queued to unload. Substantial government and private funding has since been invested here, and the port has been redeveloped as the terminal for cargo and passenger services between Merseyside and Ireland. A floating stage can work with two roll-on/roll-off ferries at the same time. Many of the fine buildings have been converted to accommodate offices, museums and apartments.

MORETON
The Roman Catholic Church c1965
M192015

Our Lady of Lourdes' Church is situated on Leasowe Road, Moreton. Built in 1957, it features a strong architectural style. Its closed appear to belie the traditional welcome one would expect from a parish church, but even in 1965 it was a brave cleric who held the doors open wide at all times.

MORETON, *Town Meadow Lane School c1965* M192021

This is not the finest example of 1960s design, but the school served an area of new housing and was probably fabricated for speed rather than aesthetics. The name Moreton is Anglo-Saxon in origin. 'More' is a corruption of mere (a lake) and 'ton' indicates a settlement. In common with much of the coastline facing the Irish Sea, the northern area of the Wirral was originally a low-lying wasteland subject to regular influx from the sea. The mere in this case would have been an area which was substantially at, or below, sea level. Land reclamation over many hundreds of years drained the mere and brought the land to a level of fertility - and latterly into habitability.

BIDSTON, *The Observatory c1950* B443001

The observatory on Bidston Hill is a recognised weather observation station. Built in 1866 by the Mersey Docks and Harbour Board to provide observations for the benefit of shipping, its records include a full set of observations dating from 1867. In the middle of the 20th century it became an adjunct of the Tidal Institute at Liverpool University, and it is now known as the Centre for Coastal and Marine Sciences - Proudman Oceanographic Laboratory.

BIDSTON, *The Windmill c1955* B443002a

Situated a few hundred yards to the south of the observatory, Bidston Mill was built at the beginning of the 19th century and was in full operation until 1875. After a period of disuse and neglect it was given new sails in 1994, and now provides an interesting centre for the area's many visitors.

UPTON
The Village c1955
U36003

UPTON
The Village c1955
U36022

UPTON, *The Cross Roads c1955*
U36010

Protected from overwhelming traffic by the encirclement of the Upton by-pass to the west and the M53 motorway to the east, Upton has changed little since these views were taken. The ownership of shops and banking establishments may have changed, but the activities of the current incumbents have stayed much the same. Teas are still being served on the corner of The Village and Arrowe Park Road at the Stone House Café (U36010, right), and the Horse and Jockey Hotel still occupies the junction of Rake Lane and The Village (U36003, left). Rose Cottage (the first full building on the right in U36003) was the local telephone exchange long before the advent of STD.

29

UPTON
*St Mary's Church
c1955* U36016

There is evidence of a Christian community in Overchurch (the original settlement, now incorporated into Upton) since AD 700-900, and a Norman church building there survived until 1813, when it was destroyed by fire. A new church was built in the centre of Upton village at a cost of £728, which in turn was replaced by the present St Mary's in 1868. The clock on the church tower was a later addition of around 1912.

UPTON
Woodlands Park c1955
U36007

Woodlands Park is a good example of that most English of urban establishments - a local rec. The properties in the background appear to be of good quality, and it is likely that parents in 1955 would have been quite happy to allow their offspring to play within sight of home. It is unlikely that the same situation prevails today.

UPTON, *Thermopylae Pass c1950* U36001

This classical referral to Greek heroics is in fact a pedestrian underpass connecting the legs of a hairpin bend in the Upton by-pass. It regularly appears in directions given to local walking groups forging a circular route from Bidston Hill. This picture is taken from Bidston Hill looking south.

UPTON
The Arrowe Park Hotel c1955 U36004

Strictly speaking, Arrowe Park Hotel is in Woodchurch to the south of Upton. Possibly the only change since the 1950s is its clientele - visually it is much the same. Nowadays it is notable for being a pub catering for young people, and probably not the place for a quiet pint of best bitter.

GREAT MEOLS
*The Railway Inn
c1955* M191032

Pandering to the needs of motorists, the first Railway Inn was pulled down in the 1930s to make way for a larger establishment. The building pictured here was opened in 1938, and its predecessor was then removed to provide a car park.

GREAT MEOLS
Birkenhead Road c1940
M191012

This view of Birkenhead Road was taken very early in the wartime decade - the parked vehicles lack the white painted edges to the front and rear wings, and none of the windows in the houses on the right show evidence of blast protection stripping that were features of the early 1940s. With four cars visible, this section of the township was obviously wealthy – indeed, it was the opening of the road link to Birkenhead that prompted the rapid growth from settlement to village.

GREAT MEOLS, *The Church of St John the Baptist c1955* M191029

The parish church of St John the Baptist was consecrated on 12 April 1913; the foundation stone had been laid eighteen months earlier. St John's present church hall was the original - and temporary - church on the site, and it opened in 1901.

GREAT MEOLS
*Station Approach
c1965* M191048

Traditionally, retail outlets built on the approaches to railway stations serving local lines have proved to be most profitable. This line-up of chemist, post office, small supermarket, ladies' wear and greengrocer/ fishmonger will have collected customers both leaving and entering the station. I imagine that the front of the newsagent/ tobacconist Is hidden behind one of the ornamental trees.

GREAT MEOLS
*The Dinghy Slipway
c1965*
M191060

GREAT MEOLS
Meols Parade c1965
M191064

It is doubtful if a more perfect example of a genteel English seafront could be found. Cars are neatly parked in driveways; visitors' vehicles are kept firmly on the other side of the municipal green and flower beds; and their owners are enjoying a quiet kick-about to break the monotony of all that water.

HOYLAKE, *Queen's Park c1965*
H277033

The park is a pleasant interlude between Birkenhead Road and Meols Parade on the seafront. When we look at this picture, it is hard to believe that Queen's Park gardens are built on levelled sand hills. The whole park is a tribute to the gardening skills of the local authority employees.

HOYLAKE
The Sands c1965 H277014

Already an endangered occupation in 1965, fishing is now in terminal decline along the whole of the north-west coastline. There has been concern for the cockle fishing in the Dee Estuary for some time, and plans are being made to severely regulate the industry. The proposed reduction in permit holders will, it is said, not only make the fishery more sustainable, but will also dramatically improve safety and reduce damage caused to the estuary.

WEST KIRBY
The Column c1965 W170041

An old mill, which was used as a navigation mark by mariners, was destroyed in a storm in 1839. Its replacement was this column, 60 feet high and bearing the following inscription: 'This column was erected by the trustees of the Liverpool Docks, by the permission of John Shaw Leigh, Esq, owner of the land, who also gave the stone for its erection, AD 1841, as a beacon for mariners frequenting the Mersey and its vicinity'.

WEST KIRBY
*The War Memorial
c1965* W170043

The view from the top
of Grange Hill over
the Dee Estuary on a
summer's day can be
quite breathtaking.
What more fitting site
for the town's war
memorial?

WEST KIRBY,
Grange Hill c1965
W170038

WEST KIRBY
The Marine Lake c1960
W170019

This superb leisure facility has a justifiable reputation for excellence. In 1960 it catered for dinghy sailors, swimmers, paddlers and canoeists, with plenty of room for all. In the 21st century it provides a venue for international wind-surfing championships.

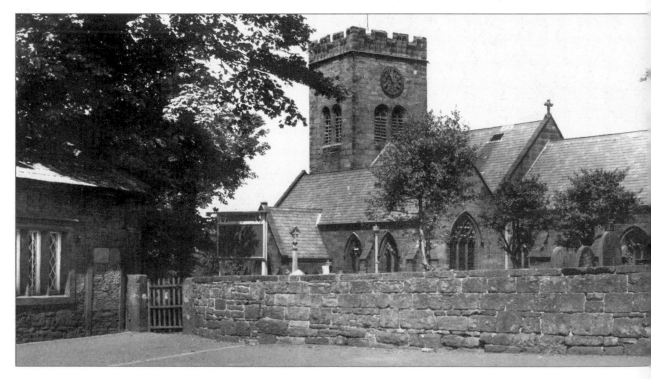

WEST KIRBY
St Bridget's Church
c1955 W170013

The first church to stand on this site was also the focal point of the Viking settlement in the 10th century. The current building has a substantial element of Norman stonework dated c1150. St Bridget's is also the modern site for two war memorials; the first a simple cross in the churchyard, complemented by the second, a beautifully carved book in the nave of the church carrying the names of the fallen.

WEST KIRBY
Banks Road
c1965
W170018

WEST KIRBY
Banks Road c1965
W170048

Banks Road and The Crescent (W170049) form the heart of the original village. There is a wide-ranging array of shops, many of them tucked away beneath the arcades. In common with so many towns on The Wirral, West Kirby is not enslaved to the usual High Street brand names and retains a remarkable measure of independence.

WEST KIRBY, *Banks Road c1965* W170061

WEST KIRBY
The Crescent 1967
W170049

Unfortunately, visitors will not find the traffic-free streets shown in our pictures. One other note of interest is the 'Cheshire black and white' decoration on many of the shop elevations.

THURSTASTON
Thor's Stone c1960
T174013

Given the Viking origins of the village, one should not be too surprised to find 'evidence' of romantic legends. Thor's Stone is a sandstone outcrop on the nearby common, a National Trust site. The Viking settlers interpreted the natural phenomenon of thunder and lightning as the god Thor striking the stone in anger with his war hammer.

THURSTASTON
St Bartholomew's Church c1955
T174007

Standing on a Christian site with a thousand-year history, this is the third church to stand in the village. A Norman building stood until 1724, a second was completed in 1824 (its tower still stands at the corner of its successor) and the third was consecrated in 1886.

THURSTASTON
A View of the Welsh Uplands c1960 T174010

Thurstaston Common is one of the highest points on the Wirral Peninsula, and an ideal vantage point to view the hills of Snowdonia across Caldy golf course and the Dee Estuary.

IRBY
*The Post Office and
The Village c1940* 142002

The eclectic mix of
architectural styles, ranging
from the thatched roof of
the single-storey old post
office and the slab-fronted
agricultural dwelling next
to it, to the generously
featured buildings
established during the first
half of the 20th century,
lend an air of long-term
solidity that was
subsequently supported by
the discovery of evidence
of both Iron Age and
Romano-British
settlements.

IRBY, *The Village c1940* 142003

IRBY
The Village c1955
142008

IRBY, *The Village c1955* 142013

This is a similar view to photograph I42002, but facing the other way and taken after a substantial interval. The thatch of the old post office has given way to slate (left), and the business itself - with its attendant telephone kiosk - has moved just a few doors down. In the 1950s the retailing element of the Cooperative movement was still popular, and Irby sports two premises on either side of the road to prove the point. An unsecured bicycle propped against the kerb (right) is a world away from the measures that would need to be taken nowadays.

HESWALL, *The Church c1955* H276044

St Peter's is a building of some antiquity, and this view of the rear of the parish church does not do justice to its clarity of line or the aesthetic appeal of its architecture. In common with most of ecclesiastical sites on the Wirral Peninsula, St Peter's can trace its origins to the original Viking settlers who established a base in West Lancashire and North Cheshire after they had been expelled from Ireland in the 10th century.

HESWALL
The View from the Church Tower c1955
H276041

The tower of the parish church is a useful vantage point, but almost fifty years of development has rendered it difficult to identify with any accuracy the buildings on the skyline across Heswall Dales. Those given to nostalgia will enjoy the sight of three hayricks (centre left, above the trees) - an agricultural technique that has been superseded by the 'Swiss roll' method of storage.

HESWALL, *A View of the Welsh Coast c1955* H276042

The view of the Welsh coastline across the Dee Estuary is almost an obligatory picture for any photographer working in West Wirral. In the intervening years there has been some housing infill, but essentially the area between church and shoreline is much as it was in 1955.

HESWALL, *The Slipway c1955* H276063

A mixture of near-derelict and beached craft gives this working slipway an untidy appearance that will certainly have been at odds with the fact that the majority of the boats represented someone's livelihood. The growth in leisure sailing, the decline in fishing as an industry, and improved access have all contributed to radical physical changes on the present use of the slipway.

DETAIL FROM H276063

HESWALL, *The Children's Hospital*
c1965 H276141

The Royal Liverpool Children's Hospital has closed since this photograph was taken. The site is now occupied by a supermarket, which may or may not have greater social benefit, and sick children are catered for at Arrowe Park Hospital, with the reassuring backup of Alder Hey in Liverpool. One can imagine that the group in the lower left of our picture is one of farewell after a short stay. The appropriately dressed Sister speaks reassuringly to mother, with an older relative (grandmother?) providing support and TLC.

DETAIL FROM H276141

HESWALL
*Telegraph Road
c1960* H276073

HESWALL
Telegraph Road c1955 H276053

The centre of Heswall was originally much closer to the shoreline, probably in the area around Village Road and St Peter's Church, but the advent of Telegraph Road - the A540 - has moved the commercial emphasis further westward. These images highlight the differences that can occur in a decade. Possibly the most obvious are the loss of the cinema on the opposite side of the road from Lloyd's Bank (H276053, in the mid distance, right) and the rebuilding of the church (H276132, right). Traffic controls are creeping in and in today's Heswall the junction is controlled by traffic lights and several miles of yellow lines. Many of the retailers in our photographs have disappeared to be replaced by fast food outlets, video rental stores and national chains. In fact, the town is one of the few in West Wirral where national brand names have made significant inroads.

HESWALL
Telegraph Road c1965
H276132

GAYTON
The Devon Doorway
c1955 G352011

Situated on the junction of Telegraph Road, Brimstage Road, Barnston Road and Chester Road, one of the busiest in West Wirral, this atmospheric pub has changed little in appearance since the picture was taken. The building actually curves into a shallow vee around the front entrance. Fame is assured by the fact that the roundabout is named after the establishment.

BARNSTON
The Fox and Hounds
c1955 B441003

The building in the picture was built c1910 on a site of an alehouse and barn; similar hostelries had stood here for almost a century. Licensing records show the Black Horse and the Sportsman's Arms as previous incarnations. In 1984 the present licensee made significant changes internally, but managed to do so without destroying any of the character of what he describes as 'a vintage thirties Wirral pub'.

BARNSTON, *Dale House Camp c1955* B441017

This picture gives an impression of a disused military establishment surplus to World War II requirements. Nothing could be further from the truth. Now over a century old, the camp is set in about 15 acres of woodland on the edge of Barnston village; as a registered charity its aim is to provide accommodation and outdoor activities for individuals and organised groups. There are sleeping facilities for 120 people, a cafe, a play area for the very young and access to some of the finest countryside the north west has to offer.

BARNSTON
The Village c1955
B441007

It is obviously a quiet time of day in this Cheshire village. The 'School' sign on the left was redundant in 1955, because the establishment had already closed; the children had been moved to a new establishment in Sandham Grove, Heswall. The building to the right of the Scott K3 telephone kiosk is probably the village post office.

BARNSTON, *The Entrance to Beech Farm c1955* B441006

Situated at the top of a steepish hill on the road from Heswall, the entrance to Beech Farm is on the right in our picture. Its claim to fame is the Barn Stone - a huge granite boulder swept down from Scotland during the last Ice Age.

BARNSTON
Tree Cottage c1955 B441001

Tree Cottage appears to be a substantial property, possibly the home of a senior agricultural worker or land agent. The attached outbuildings are obviously well maintained, as opposed to the rather ramshackle appearance of those opposite, and this suggests a long-term occupation of the house. It is possible that the building has undergone a change of both ownership and name during the past fifty years, since there is no longer any recorded trace of a Barnston property with this title.

THORNTON HOUGH
The Entrance to Thornton Manor c1950 T221005

The industrialist and philanthropist William Lever moved into Thornton Manor in 1888. As Lord Leverhulme he made the property his family home. On his death in 1925, he was succeeded by his son and grandson, and, when the latter died in July 2000 without a male heir, his death prompted the sale of Thornton Manor and all its contents. The former Leverhulme home is now an exclusive hotel and health spa.

EASTHAM
Queen Elizabeth II Docks c1955 E9021

The locks and docks at Eastham form the western end of the Manchester Ship Canal. The Queen Elizabeth II Dock - specially designed to handle bulk liquid petroleum products, chemicals and edible oils - can accommodate vessels of up to 40,000 tonnes deadweight and a draught of up to 10 metres. In 2002 the dock handled nearly 887,000 tonnes of product. It is regrettable that nothing was known of the two vessels pictured here, the 'Languedoc' and the 'Dauphine', despite close questioning of older employees at Eastham.

EASTHAM, *The Church and Church Lane c1955* E9006

Many visitors come to admire the beauty of St Mary's Church. The original church was built in the 12th century. Parts of the first tower remain integral with the present church, which dates from 1574. A yew tree in the churchyard has been certified by dendrologists to be over one thousand years old.

EASTHAM
Eastham Rake
c1955 E9033

EASTHAM, *Bridle Road c1955* E9032

Running at right angles to each other, Eastham Rake and Bridle Road link at the junction with Stanley Lane and the A41 - New Chester Road. Far from maintaining the sort of quietude suggested here, today both are major access roads to local public transport, the oil storage installation and the beautiful Country Park. Generations of residents have worked to remove traffic from the narrow, winding village streets and the main road to Chester ran through the village until the by-pass was built in the 1930s. Recently the local authority has authorised additional traffic calming measures to be placed at the junctions of the by-pass with Village Road - the B5132 - as drivers use the old road to avoid congestion and forget their road manners as they progress.

BROMBOROUGH
The Cross c1965
B445011

BROMBOROUGH, *The Cross c1965* B445018

In contrast with the western side of the Wirral Peninsula, the towns and villages of the east have become one continuous conurbation because of their proximity to the River Mersey and Liverpool. Regrettably the village of Bromborough entered into the changes with some alacrity, particularly in the years immediately before and after the First World War; almost all traces of ancient Bromborough were destroyed. Bromborough Cross is one of the few things that remain, but even this is not completely original. The base and steps are probably late 13th century and the top was added in 1874.

BROMBOROUGH
Raby Mere c1955
B445006

The proximity of the M53 motorway has removed some of the peace from the surroundings of Raby Mere, but the wildlife continues to flourish, and visitors continue to enjoy a wide variety of country pursuits. The associated Raby Hall contains a centre operated by Wirral Autistic Society. Close to both is the Wheatsheaf Inn, a half-timbered hostelry that has dispensed hospitality since 1611.

BEBINGTON, *Wirral Grammar School for Boys c1955* B660014a

In 1955 the Grammar School would have been in preparation for its 25th anniversary the following year. Under modern educational administration, this leading establishment is a selective foundation school catering for 11- to 18-year-olds. This photograph was taken during high summer (note the open windows), but we wonder how many of today's pupils have ever seen Cross Lane so devoid of traffic at any time of year.

BEBINGTON, *Mayer Hall c1965*
B660051

Mayer Hall commemorates the life and works of Joseph Mayer, the 19th-century antiquary and book collector who made his home in Bebington. The building now houses a selection of municipal offices, a small art gallery, and community service groups. The floral bed to the left of the picture highlights the work of the Women's Voluntary Service before that organisation received royal recognition and became the WRVS.

DETAIL FROM B660051

BEBINGTON
Church Road
c1965 B660056

BEBINGTON, *Bebington Road c1965* B660057

These pictures highlight the benefits of a variety of small shops serving a close community. No need for the weekly trek to the supermarket and the massive loading of container-sized quantities of groceries into the car; just a short walk to collect what you need for a couple of days. The growth of out-of-town sites has rendered such areas almost redundant, and few of the retailers in these photographs are still in business.

BEBINGTON
*Higher Bebington
Road c1955* B660041

For all its evocative
name, Higher
Bebington Road is
quite short in length; it
services Bebington
High Sports College,
the Higher Bebington
recreation ground and
the local branch of
Wirral Libraries.
Apparently constructed
just after World War II,
the road surface is
composed of the
ubiquitous concrete
slab. There are so many
of these on the Wirral
that one has to imagine
a lurking machine of
titanic proportions,
together with its
attendants, waiting to
be fed large quantities
of cement and
aggregate to spread on
any surface not
otherwise occupied.

BEBINGTON
*Heath Road
c1960* B660048

Linking Lower
and Higher
Bebington, Heath
Road also forms
one boundary of
the Wirral
Grammar Schools
site. The open
space on the
right-hand side of
the road marks
the playing fields
of a local primary
school.

BEBINGTON, *Spital Cross Roads c1965* B660064

This important road junction makes possible an alternative traffic flow between Bebington and Bromborough, and between the M53 motorway and New Chester Road (the A41). The Three Stags on the corner with Church Road (left) is now designated a Big Steak Pub. Not the place for a quiet pint, then.

PORT SUNLIGHT
The Fountain and Lady Lever Art Gallery c1965 P188099

Designed by W & S Owen and built between 1913 and 1922, this memorial to the life of Lady Lever has brought pleasure to millions. The building is a simple design in Portland stone that contrasts well with Port Sunlight village. It has been quoted as being 'probably the best surviving example of late Victorian and Edwardian taste'. It is also the only major public urban gallery built by its founder to house the collection he had assembled for it.

PORT SUNLIGHT, *The Leverhulme Memorial c1965* P188102

Impressive as this memorial to Viscount Leverhulme is, it should not be forgotten that there is another, and a very live one, on the Western Isles. In the course of planning for retirement, Lord Leverhulme bought land in the Western Isles on Lewis and Harris. However, instead of retirement, this move led to his setting up of another company and plans to improve the economy of the islands and the lives of the people living there. In 1922 he was made a Viscount, and became Viscount Leverhulme of the Western Isles. His Scottish ventures were partially successful, but he eventually sold his land to the local population in 1923. Today the Leverhulme Memorial School is thriving on the Isle of Harris.

PORT SUNLIGHT
Bolton Road Bowling Green c1965 P188079

Bolton Road was the first paved road laid in Port Sunlight, and W H Lever named it after his home town as a reminder of his roots. Bowls is a quintessentially English sporting activity, and it appealed to the founder of the project. The houses at the back of the green are a perfect illustration of the architectural style that has made Port Sunlight so famous.

PORT SUNLIGHT
The Bridge Inn c1955
P188030

The building was designed to resemble an old English coaching inn; it was named after the Victoria Bridge over the original estuary. Rendered in colour-washed roughcast, and with large overhanging half-timbered gables, the U-shaped building encloses a spacious forecourt. Inside, the refurbished oak-panelled dining area only gives an indication of the splendour of the original decoration. As a strict teetotaller W H Lever at first refused to allow strong liquor to be served, but relented after strong persuasion from his workforce. The first licence was granted in1903.

PORT SUNLIGHT
Christ Church c1960 P188096

Designed again by W & S Owen, the parish church is built of Helsby sandstone in the Gothic manner. Although it has unremarkable proportions, these help it to blend perfectly into the setting of the village. Christ Church was consecrated in 1904.

PORT SUNLIGHT
Dell Bridge and the Lyceum c1955
P188036

Although originally known as the Schools, the building has had a variety of uses - a men's social club, an evening institute and a Christian meeting place. It was renamed after it became a Staff Training College. Designed by Douglas and Fordham, it was opened in 1894, and was one of the buildings of which Lever was most proud.

PORT SUNLIGHT
Hulme Hall c1955
P188031

Hulme Hall began life as a women's dining hall, and now plays host to a variety of social functions, minor exhibitions and fairs. For a time the building housed the Lever family's growing art collection before its eventual removal to Thornton Manor. In common with many other public buildings in the village, the gabled exterior hides an ornate interior.

OXTON, *The Caernarvon Castle and St Saviour's Church c1960* O90002

The old village custom of placing the pub next to the church is not overlooked in Oxton. St Saviour's also supports a church-aided primary school, and both are a power in the community. And while the architecture of the Castle does not exactly gel with that of the church, both buildings attract their fair share of visitors at the appropriate times.

OXTON
Arno Park c1955 O90012

Our picture shows Arno Park at its best, and showing evidence of the best of care and attention. Unfortunately, fifty years later the area is the subject of attention from the police, as gangs of young men and women make life difficult for local residents.

BIRKENHEAD
Arrowe Park c1960
B399020

BIRKENHEAD
Arrowe Park c1960 B399022

To celebrate the 21st anniversary of the founding of the Scout Movement, 56,000 scouts from around the world held their 3rd International Jamboree in Arrowe Park. A campsite of 450 acres was provided free of charge by the then Birkenhead Corporation. The site was a mile long by half a mile broad, and the scouts of all nationalities camped together. Today the park is better known for its involvement with the NHS on the Wirral. The purpose-built Arrowe Park Hospital today has some 920 beds; it offers A & E services to the whole of the Peninsula, and admits as many as 140 emergency patients on a busy day.

BIRKENHEAD, *Storeton Road 1954* B399007

A pub of the old school where the landlord caters for everyone from 18 to 80, the Halfway House (right) has been in continuous operation since 1893. The junction has been improved to cope with modern traffic flows, but the area in general has changed but little in 50 years.

BIRKENHEAD
Hamilton Square c1955
B399030

Hamilton Square was completed in 1826. It has the largest number of Grade I listed buildings in one place in England, with the exception of Trafalgar Square in London. The large building across the square is Birkenhead Town Hall. The white block in front of it is the town's war memorial. The monument in the centre was modelled on the original Eleanor Cross, which was erected by King Edward I - he twice visited Birkenhead Priory.

BIRKENHEAD
Charing Cross c1965
B399043

With five roads feeding into it, this famous junction (close to the access to the Queensway Tunnel under the River Mersey) is one of the busiest in the region. Much has changed since 1965. Traffic control measures mean that there is almost no legal parking in the area. The Midland Bank (right) is now a wine bar, and the Grange Hotel (left) is now known as the Charing Cross. Shop fronts have tumbled, and the 'global' names have moved in, as they have in most other large shopping areas.

BIRKENHEAD
The Queensway Tunnel c1965 B399027

The first of the road traffic tunnels to be dug under the River Mersey, the Queensway Tunnel was opened by King George V and Queen Mary on 18 July 1934. Some 200,000 people gathered to watch the event - and 80,000 of those celebrated with a 'tunnel walk' through from Liverpool to Birkenhead. Presumably they also walked back. The tunnel entrance has undergone minor modifications since the 1960s, but it is still recognisable from our picture.

THE
NORTHERN
SHORE

LIVERPOOL
The Ferry Boats c1955 L60021

The Mersey ferries are world-famous, even without a boost from pop music, and no printed coverage of the city would be complete unless homage was paid to these links with the Wirral Peninsula. Although the vehicle ferries were made redundant when the Queensway tunnel was opened, foot passenger traffic continued unabated until the opening of the Kingsway tunnel coincided with a universal franchise in car ownership. In modern Liverpool the ferries are almost as busy as before, but this time with leisure traffic and pleasure trips.

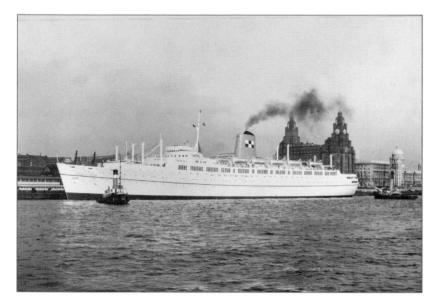

LIVERPOOL
The 'Empress of England' c1958
L60034

The 'Empress of England' was built in 1957 by Vickers-Armstrong of Newcastle. Originally intended to run the liner service from Liverpool to Quebec and Montreal in summer and Liverpool to Saint John's in winter, she began to spend her winters cruising in the Caribbean from New York as air travel hit the Atlantic market. Sold to Shaw Savill in 1970, she underwent an over-long refit at Cammell Laird, and in so doing missed a vital slot in the cruising schedules from which she never recovered. Renamed as the 'Ocean Monarch', she operated for a further four years before being sold for scrap in 1975.

LIVERPOOL, *Ranelagh Street c1950* L60033

Named after the 17th-century London pleasure gardens, Ranelagh Street provides an important link between Lime Street and the now pedestrianised shopping centre to the north of Hanover Street. It also accesses the equally important Central Station junction (right), where the Wirral and Northern local rail lines interconnect. The station concourse now houses a small shopping centre, and the entrance has been relocated to halfway between the sign shown in the picture and Lime Street. Almost all of the shops have changed hands in the intervening years, some several times; but the eclectic mix remains, to the benefit of shoppers drawn to the area.

LIVERPOOL
Booker Avenue
c1955 L60017

LIVERPOOL, *Booker Avenue from Holmefield Road c1955* L60018

Located in the suburb of Allerton, this junction provides access to West Allerton train station and to the B5180 and A562 arterial roads. As such it sees increasing amounts of road traffic to the detriment of the local infrastructure, including the shops in the photograph. None of them now exhibit the smart appearance they had in the 1950s, and it would not be wise to park bicycles en masse without providing some form of additional security. The post office has closed, but another is now located half-a-mile away in Melbreck Road.

LIVERPOOL
Walton Village c1955 W16025

Now a single-carriageway 'blip' delaying the progress of traffic using the A580 urban route to Goodison Park (the home of Everton FC) and the city centre, Walton Village has not resembled this picture in many years. Limited road widening has removed most of the identifiable features of this photograph, and it would be either a very brave or a very foolhardy photographer who attempted to obtain a 21st-century update.

DETAIL FROM W16025

THE
COASTAL
STRIP

CROSBY, *Marine Gardens c1960* C357004

The backdrop of houses in Marine Crescent and Marine Terrace show little of the passing years as the 'greening' of the protective sands between them and Crosby Marina adds to the pleasant outlook. Within the immediate vicinity there are ample leisure facilities for those whose interests lie outside sailing: athletics, pitch and putt, tennis, soccer, rugby football and a fitness centre complete with a swimming pool are all available locally.

CROSBY
Myers Road East
c1965 C357009

Located in an area of high-density housing, the shops at this junction continue to provide a vital service to residents. The identities of the majority of the owners have changed, as one would expect, but the mix remains much the same, and reflects the needs of the customers.

CROSBY, *The Merchant Taylors School c1960* C357010

Founded in 1620, the Merchant Taylors Schools in Crosby operate in similar fashion to old-style grammar schools, but under links with the charitable governance of the Merchant Taylors Company in London. While boys and girls are taught separately, the educational organisation for both is similar, with Junior, Lower and Middle Schools and a Sixth Form. A number of improvements since the 1960s have resulted in a changed appearance of the buildings in our photograph, but the visual essence remains much as we see here.

CROSBY
The Windmill c1960
C357017

Substantial tree growth has filled the gaps around the dwelling house in our picture, and the height of the trees has rendered the windmill barely visible from Moor Lane. Crosby Mill is a good example of a tower mill, a design that appeared after the post mill was established. These cylindrical-shaped mills were usually made of stone or brick, with walls at least 18 inches thick; a revolving cap brought the sails into the wind. The outer walls were plastered over or tarred in order to keep moisture out, and it was necessary for the mill to be cylindrical in shape so that the sails could clear the face of the tower.

CROSBY
*Moor Lane
By-Pass c1960*
C357016

BLUNDELLSANDS, *The Roman Catholic Church c1960* B444009

St Joseph's Church has served the Catholic community in Blundellsands since the building was consecrated in 1874. In this very settled community, very little has happened during the past forty years to change the appearance of either the building or its surroundings. In common wlth many other villages in the area, the incorporation of the word 'Blundell' into the place name is a reminder of the extent of the Blundell family's influence during the 18th and 19th centuries.

BLUNDELLSANDS
The Blundellsands Hotel c1960
B444001

Once one of the must-be-seen locations in the area, the hotel was sold at the turn of the 20th century; it has been converted into a retirement apartment complex with a restaurant, a conservatory, a hobbies room and a guest suite.

BLUNDELLSANDS
The Beach c1960
B444014

BLUNDELLSANDS
The Beach c1960
B444010

BLUNDELLSANDS
Crosby Baths c1960 B444021

Blundellsands beach forms part of the sixteen miles of sand stretching from Waterloo to Southport. Immediately beyond Blundellsands, however, visitors should be aware of the dangers posed by the proximity of the military ranges at Altcar. The local authority has formed the intention to create the Crosby Coastal Park stretching as far as the River Alt at Hightown. Part of the planning includes the assimilation of the site of the now-demolished Crosby Baths.

FORMBY
The Village c1960 F106013

As a barometer of Formby's growth in the second half of the 20th century, Chapel Lane (facing us) is a good measuring device. Many of the shops on both right and left had only recently been, or were yet to be, converted from private dwelling houses. The paved areas in front of those in the picture are the erstwhile front gardens of the houses, and the architecture above the shop fronts also betrays the origins of the buildings. Martins Bank (right) was acquired by Barclays in 1969. The elms on the left of Chapel Lane were removed in 1975 because of the ravages of Dutch elm disease. The roundabout has now been joined by several traffic-calming devices to cope with traffic volume, and at the beginning of the new millennium a set of pedestrian-operated traffic lights was installed halfway along this busy shopping street.

FORMBY
The Town Centre c1960
F106008

We have taken a 90-degree turn from F106013, and we face the opposite view of the corner of Chapel Lane and Three Tuns Lane. The site of Goodwood Furnishing (right) was originally occupied by the Rimmer family's fish, game and poultry outlets, and it is now home to a branch of Lloyds TSB Bank in a purpose-built block. The shop immediately beyond it is a hardware shop, and remains so today. To the left of the picture is the site of the Formby war memorial; behind it was property owned by the Catholic church, now occupied by a supermarket and its car park.

FORMBY
The Post Office and the Village c1955 F106003

At the opposite end of Chapel Lane stands the post office (left), which originally offered a full counter service, but is now relegated to sorting and parcels distribution. The timbered building beyond is a branch of the National Westminster Bank, and the properties beyond that have all been demolished in the interests of building mundane blocks of shops. On the right-hand side of the road the shops in view and all beyond it have been similarly redeveloped.

FORMBY
The Recreation Ground c1960
F106009

Duke Street 'rec' has lost its thatched maintenance building, and the surface underneath the swings now conforms to several health and safety regulations, none of which could possibly be as effective as the sand in our picture. Fortunately, modern children continue to enjoy themselves in the same way as children have always done. The recreation ground is also home to a weekend junior soccer league.

FORMBY
The Beach c1960
F106019

An enduring pleasure for residents and visitors alike, the beach at Formby Point is a sensitive area in terms of its ecology. There are a number of examples of flora and fauna which are unique to the dunes and the pine woods – this landscape is the legacy of the days when the whole area was a sea-washed patchwork of sand and marsh. Cars are no longer welcome on the beach, and there are car parks provided by the local authority and the National Trust.

FORMBY, *The Old Lifeboat House c1965* F106030

Records show that Formby was the site of the first lifeboat station in the British Isles. There are no images of the original building, but a decision by Liverpool Town Council in 1776 established the necessity for it on the basis that the North Meols coastline was deemed dangerous to shipping. The lifeboat house in the photograph was decommissioned in 1918. Used as a cafe for many years, it was eventually demolished in 1965.

FRESHFIELD
Rye Ground Lane c1965
F117001

Freshfield was established as the name for the railway station located between Formby and Ainsdale: it was built on a field owned by Mr Fresh. It can be argued that the view in the picture forms the gateway to the area, which is considered by many to be a highly desirable location for a home. The Grapes Hotel (left) was built c1880, and in its original form included assembly rooms and a brewhouse. The junction is now notorious for its off-centre mini-roundabout. In 1998 it was carefully refurbished and the cobbles forming the 'bump' were carefully corrected - to be even further out of alignment.

FRESHFIELD
Old Town Lane Post Office c1965
F117018

An unusual, but often most welcome, combination of pharmacy and sub-post office, the building on the near left has performed the function under at least three owners to the knowledge of the author. Old Town Lane is the route between the new village centre and the original village. The latter was inundated by sand and sea in the 18th century, and a new settlement was established a mile or so inland. The buildings beyond the pharmacy, a butcher's in 1965, are now a doctor's surgery.

FRESHFIELD
Gores Lane c1965 F117003

One of the most important cross-village links, Gores Lane appears under one guise or another on all the oldest maps of Formby. Its original value lay in the number of farms and steadings that lay on its route, but its main function today is to provide a relief from the traffic on roads closer to the east of the village. Wilson's Garage (centre) was the first to be established in Formby - although not on this particular site. In the early days of private aviation, the company's founder Tom Wilson often serviced the string-and-sealing-wax aircraft flown by the pioneers who used Freshfield beach as a landing strip. The garage has now been supplanted by private homes.

FRESHFIELD, *Victoria Buildings c1965* F117002

Very little has changed in these shops, which were built immediately opposite Freshfield station. The mix of ownership and business is much the same as in 1965; only the trees show signs of the passing years. The level crossing gates (right) have now been replaced with automatic rising barriers, and the signal box has been demolished.

FRESHFIELD
The Formby Golf Club c1965 F117020

Formed in 1884 as a private club for just 25 members, the Formby course has played host to an increasing number of national and international tournaments in recent years. A neighbouring Freshfield Club existed until World War II, when the land was requisitioned as a Royal Air Force station and the clubhouse became the Officers' Mess.

AINSDALE
The Sandhills c1965 A174002

In common with the rest of this coastline, the sand dunes now constitute the major defence against incursion by the sea. The sand itself is contained, more or less, by strong-rooted grass (mainly marram or star grass). However, it has been accepted that the natural movement of the coastline cannot be halted unless it be at an unacceptable cost to the taxpayer for the benefit of very few. Ainsdale still allows motor vehicles to park on the beach for a small charge. The author can recommend the area as a perfect spot for viewing and photographing some of the most spectacular sunsets in the country.

DETAIL FROM A174002

AINSDALE
The Lido c1965 A174006

Despite a number of attempts at regeneration, the Lido at Ainsdale was an early casualty of the national move to overseas holidays. However, a lifeline has recently been thrown in the form of the development of wind-powered sports such as kite surfing, kite flying, landboarding, kite buggies and blokarting on the nearby beach. If the activities prove as popular as they are expected to, there are

plans to develop Ainsdale Lido into a visitor centre, shop and training facility. During World War II the Lido was temporarily known as HMS Queen Charlotte (1941 to 1946), when it was used as the base for a naval anti-aircraft gunnery school.

AINSDALE, *The Roundabout c1965* A174025

We are exiting Station Road, and this townscape has changed greatly in forty years. The site of the garage (centre right) is still devoted to the motor vehicle, although now as a very large fuel station and convenience store. To its left (in the direction of Southport), the Plaza Cinema has now been replaced by the Natterjack pub and carvery restaurant. The houses on the extreme left are something of an anachronism, because they are surrounded by neighbourhood shops; one has to assume that only the stubbornness of a succession of owners has enabled them to survive commercial pressures.

AINSDALE
Station Road c1965
A174029

Station Road, though quite short in length, still manages to achieve a broad mix of shops and dwelling houses. The left-hand side of the road shows some evidence of renewal building in the slab-fronted style of the shops in the middle distance. Unlike Formby village, there is little evidence of homes being converted to shops here.

AINSDALE, *Station Road c1965* A174034

SOUTHPORT
Lord Street c1955 S160038

'A town built for pleasure' is possibly the best description for Southport. It grew from the humble beginnings of a bathing shelter on the border of North Meols into the sizeable conurbation depicted here. Lord Street was built as a boulevard shopping street with fine canopied pavements - a place to see and be seen - and it is still an aspirational goal for many national retail chain stores. Traffic lights linked to pedestrian crossings now control most of the junctions along the street; a policeman controlling traffic is a rare sight indeed. The ladies' wear shop on the corner of Nevill Street (on the left) is now a national footwear retailer, but the facades of that and its neighbour have been refurbished recently and continue to present an imposing image.

SOUTHPORT, *Lord Street c1960* S160127

SOUTHPORT
The Children's Zoo c1955 S160056

One of the resort's more enduring pleasures, the children's section of Southport Zoo truly gave happiness to many hundreds of thousands. The site was closed in 2004 under the pressures of changing regulations and the activities of animal rights activists. In truth, the attraction had probably had its day. It was time to move on.

SOUTHPORT
The Floral Hall Colonnade c1955 S160007

The Floral Hall and Theatre complex continue to provide a conference and concert centre of national importance. The years have treated the buildings kindly, and a major refurbishment at the turn of the century ensures their continuing popularity. Our picture provides no surprises in the context of 2004 - although a visitor should not expect to see the ladies in the audience wearing hats. Some of the garden area nearest to the camera has undergone modification as part of the very large project involving the building of the new Marine Parade Bridge.

SOUTHPORT
New Bridge and Marine Bridge
c1955 S160009

Built to link the Promenade to the attractions of Princes Park, the doubly-named bridge rests on two artificial islands in the Marine Lake. It provides an open-air stage for a number of annual events - not least the spectacular fireworks competition held at the end of the school holiday period. The present foreground view remains similar to this picture, but the area between the far side of the lake and the shore has been transformed by the buildings of the Ocean Plaza retail and entertainment development.

SOUTHPORT
The Pier
c1955
S160114

SOUTHPORT, *The Pier Train c1960* S160197

Obviously still viable in these photographs, Southport Pier was closed in the 1990s; it was demolished and rebuilt at a total cost of £7 million, and was reopened in 2002. Similarly the Marine Parade Bridge, part of which is visible in S160114, suffered years of neglect; it was closed to the public, and has very recently been replaced. The buildings at the pierhead are typical of their day, and so are their modern counterparts of the hopefully-named 'Funland'. The pier now has a road-train purely for the purpose of transporting those who might find the full length a little taxing.

SOUTHPORT
The Promenade, Looking North c1960 S160155

In traffic-congestion terms much closer to the Southport of today, this photograph was taken at the height of the summer season. Several sets of traffic lights control the flow of vehicles now, and it is rare to find a queue such as this. The pierhead buildings have been demolished and rebuilt since 1960, and the opening of the new Marine Parade Bridge has considerably altered the outlook. At the far end of the Promenade, the old hospital buildings are being redeveloped as luxury homes.

DETAIL FROM S160155

CHURCHTOWN
Botanic Road c1950
C714009

CHURCHTOWN, *Botanic Road c1960* C714020

Churchtown can trace its recorded history back to the Viking landings, but it is also true that the settlement will have been in existence before the outcasts from Ireland made their way ashore. Development was slow and gradual as the inhabitants dragged a poor existence from the sea and the land. They lived in a cluster of mud-daubed cottages built of wreck timber close to the walls of the church - hence Church Town. It should be appreciated that the sea was considerably closer than the modern shoreline, so that in the Middle Ages sea fishing became the all-important industry in the area.

CHURCHTOWN
Botanic Road c1965 C714044

The little township expanded westwards, with homes inside the banks erected to keep the sea at bay. Many of the smaller houses in the Churchtown locale owe their beginnings to shrimpers' and fishermen's cottages. Although the shops shown in the photographs are still in operation, the ownership has changed many times. Churchtown is now a much sought-after location for a home, retaining, as it does, an air of gentility and respectability that has disappeared from many parts of its noisy neighbour.

CHURCHTOWN, *Cambridge Road c1950* C714011

CHURCHTOWN
*The Hesketh Arms Hotel
c1960* C714025

Standing on the site of what were once three fishermen's cottages, the Hesketh Arms was originally called the Black Bull. William 'Duke' Sutton was landlord of the Black Bull when he opened his bathing hut at South Hawes near what is now the junction of Duke Street and Lord Street. He later built the original hotel near the site, suffering it to be known as 'Duke's Folly'. South Hawes later became known as South Port, which eventually became Southport.

CHURCHTOWN, *The Bold Arms Hotel c1960* C714026

Formerly known as the Griffin, the Bold Arms takes its name and heraldic device from one of the two families that owned most of North Meols for many centuries. Stables to the rear of the pub were used for the horses drawing the first trams in the area. The site of the tram sheds is also to the rear of the building.

CHURCHTOWN, *St Cuthbert's Church c1965* C714040

The relics of St Cuthbert are alleged to have rested in twelve places, in what is now Lancashire, during the 9th century. One was identified as Mele (an alternative spelling of Meol), and in accordance with the custom of the day, an eponymous house of prayer was raised in the saint's honour. St Cuthbert's, Churchtown is reputed to date back to pre-Conquest times, but there is no evidence to support this. The present building was raised in stone in 1571 and rebuilt between 1730 and 1739. The tower and surmounting spire were refurbished in 1850. The Conservative Club is housed in what was once the Grammar School. Built in 1729, it became a National School in 1826. The school itself moved to a new building in 1889 when it became known as St Cuthbert's Church of England School. Appropriately enough, Churchtown's present primary school is sited close by, retaining a scholastic connection despite the passing of many years.

CHURCHTOWN
The Entrance to the Botanic Gardens c1965
C714024

Originally opened in November 1874, the Botanic Gardens were designed as 'a place with an almost endless variety of attractions'; admission was 4d. The lake was formed from the old Otter Pool, which was reputedly the source of eels for the monks who lived in the area of the township. Southport local authority came to the rescue in 1932, when financial difficulties were about to force a sale to a housing development company. Refurbished and divided into a park and playing fields, the gardens were reopened in August 1937 as the Botanic Gardens and King George Playing Fields.

THE INLAND STRETCH

ST HELENS, *The Town Hall c1955* S415003

St Helens was only a small village until the advent of the Industrial Revolution. Coal mining had been a major industry regionally since the 16th century; the coal had traditionally been transported by packhorse into neighbouring Cheshire and to Liverpool. With the construction of the Sankey Canal Navigation in 1762, the town became ideally placed to transport coal nationwide. Many new industries emerged, not least of which was Pilkington Brothers. They became famous internationally for the manufacture of glass, an industry that is still closely associated with the modern town. By 1868 the town had become significant enough to be granted the status of Municipal Borough, and in 1884 it sent its first Member to Parliament. The wealth of the Victorian town can be gauged from the magnificence of its Town Hall in Victoria Square. Now subject to all the problems associated with the growth of car ownership, it is unlikely that a policeman still carries out point duty in the Square.

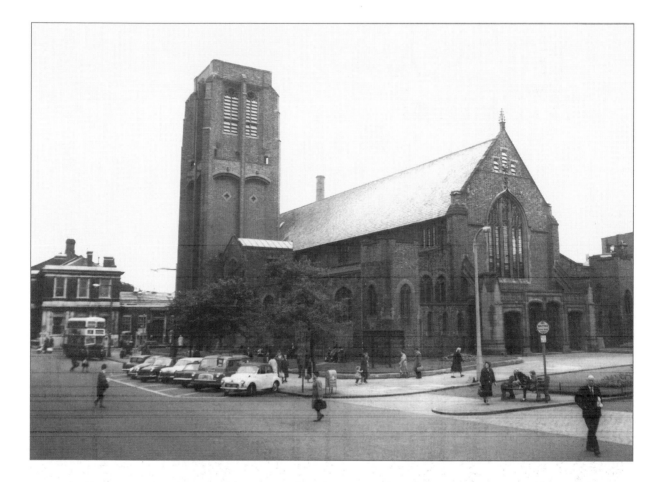

ST HELENS, *The Parish Church c1965* S415031

The town of St Helens derives its name from the early chapel dedicated to the saint. It was situated at the crossroads between the early settlements that we now know as Warrington, Widnes, Prescot and Wigan. The first known reference to the chapel was found in a document of 1552, though the original structure probably dated back to the 14th century. The modern church of St Helen was only completed in 1926, on or near the site of the early chapel. It is an evangelical church, and the present clergy are noted for taking their message out into the nearby shopping centre.

ST HELENS
Church Street c1965
S415040

The proximity of these busy shopping streets to the new Church Square shopping centre has brought some gold and some dross to the town. Many of the major stores have moved into prime positions, others have taken advantage of the pedestrianisation of Church Street to cast long shadows. The overhead trolley wires in Church Street were removed long ago.

ST HELENS, *Church Street c1965* S415005

ST HELENS
Ormskirk Street c1965
S415035

Apart from the national names such as Boots, Woolworth's and Marks & Spencer, none of the stores shown in these photographs of Church Street and Ormskirk Street have survived into the 21st century. Multi-storey car parks have removed the vehicles from the streets.

ST HELENS, *Ormskirk Street c1965* S415023

EARLESTOWN
Earle Street c1965
E218013

EARLESTOWN
Nine Arches and the Canal c1955 E218002

Solid evidence of Victorian endeavour and values, Stephenson's great viaduct carries the Liverpool/Manchester railway over the Sankey Canal. The juxtaposition of factories, railway and canal give the strongest indication of the prosperity that accrued to this area in the 18th, 19th and first half of the 20th centuries. It is worth reflecting that the two forms of transport - water and rail - were not, at first, incompatible. Later the growth of the commercial road vehicle industry was to deal a killer blow to them both.

EARLESTOWN
The Parade c1965 E218014

The Co-operative movement has its roots in north west England, and these pictures illustrate well its position in this community. A few years earlier, one local commentator had written: 'the other side [of Earle Street] has been considerably improved with the growth of the local Co-operative Society. The large central premises have taken the place of some old one-storey shops; the new butchery department and offices take the place of a small brick hutment shop with the addition of a butcher's shop and house which stood there'.

EARLESTOWN
Market Street c1960 E218005

Here and above we see contrasting aspects of one of the town's most important thoroughfares: a quiet residential section overlooked by the comforting bulk of the Town Hall, and the busy shopping area where the opportunity is often presented to meet and greet friends and neighbours in addition to purchasing life's necessities. The young mother on the right is probably a grandmother by now, and does not remember the quality of the Silver Cross perambulator that carried her pride and joy in 1960. Some of the names above the shop windows are still with us, but certainly not occupying the same premises.

EARLESTOWN
Market Street
c1955 E218003

EARLESTOWN
The Market c1960
E218010

The Market is still very
much a part of modern
life, and fulfils its prime
function on six days of
every week.

NEWTON-LE-WILLOWS, *High Street c1955* N149004

NEWTON-LE-WILLOWS, *High Street c1960* N149028

NEWTON-LE-WILLOWS, *High Street c1965* N149033

These opposing views of the High Street are photographed at five year intervals. They show a quite surprising use of private cars - an indication of the prosperity of the town - but very few pedestrians. This may be due to the time of day or the fact that Newton's High Street was already losing its importance to the local economy, even in 1955. The relevance of two fish and chip shops sited directly opposite the Pied Bull pub needs no further comment, but one has to question the suitability of the branch of a national bank - apparently located in two converted houses - being situated next door to the simplicity of a local B&B. The enduring presence of the parish church of St Peter adds timelessness to the scene.

NEWTON-LE-WILLOWS
Leigh Arms Corner c1965 N149032

These photographs are not an opportunity to comment on the drinking habits of Newtonians, but an interesting study in contrasting styles in licensed premises - road house, local welcome, and solid respectability. The intervening years have recorded very few subsequent changes in the appearance of these buildings - apart from some adjustments to their exterior décor.

NEWTON-LE-WILLOWS
The Pied Bull c1960
N149027

NEWTON-LE-WILLOWS
The Oak Tree Hotel c1960
N149023

NEWTON-LE-WILLOWS
Crow Lane East c1960 N149024

Another of the town's important roads, Crow Lane East was extended in the 1960s with the addition of a library, the original Technical School and a large estate of social housing. Now much busier than portrayed in our picture, this junction has acquired all the additional street furniture that is apparently so vital to a modern lifestyle. What would the 21st century make of the blatant cigarette advertising?

DETAIL FROM N149024

INDEX

Frith Book Co Titles

www.francisfrith.co.uk

The Frith Book Company publishes over 100 new titles each year. A selection of those currently available is listed below. For latest catalogue please contact Frith Book Co.
Town Books 96 pages, approximately 100 photos. **County and Themed Books** 128 pages, approximately 150 photos (unless specified). All titles hardback with laminated case and jacket, except those indicated pb (paperback)

Amersham, Chesham & Rickmansworth (pb)	1-85937-340-2	£9.99	Devon (pb)	1-85937-297-x	£9.99
Andover (pb)	1-85937-292-9	£9.99	Devon Churches (pb)	1-85937-250-3	£9.99
Aylesbury (pb)	1-85937-227-9	£9.99	Dorchester (pb)	1-85937-307-0	£9.99
Barnstaple (pb)	1-85937-300-3	£9.99	Dorset (pb)	1-85937-269-4	£9.99
Basildon Living Memories (pb)	1-85937-515-4	£9.99	Dorset Coast (pb)	1-85937-299-6	£9.99
Bath (pb)	1-85937-419-0	£9.99	Dorset Living Memories (pb)	1-85937-584-7	£9.99
Bedford (pb)	1-85937-205-8	£9.99	Down the Severn (pb)	1-85937-560-x	£9.99
Bedfordshire Living Memories	1-85937-513-8	£14.99	Down The Thames (pb)	1-85937-278-3	£9.99
Belfast (pb)	1-85937-303-8	£9.99	Down the Trent	1-85937-311-9	£14.99
Berkshire (pb)	1-85937-191-4	£9.99	East Anglia (pb)	1-85937-265-1	£9.99
Berkshire Churches	1-85937-170-1	£17.99	East Grinstead (pb)	1-85937-138-8	£9.99
Berkshire Living Memories	1-85937-332-1	£14.99	East London	1-85937-080-2	£14.99
Black Country	1-85937-497-2	£12.99	East Sussex (pb)	1-85937-606-1	£9.99
Blackpool (pb)	1-85937-393-3	£9.99	Eastbourne (pb)	1-85937-399-2	£9.99
Bognor Regis (pb)	1-85937-431-x	£9.99	Edinburgh (pb)	1-85937-193-0	£8.99
Bournemouth (pb)	1-85937-545-6	£9.99	England In The 1880s	1-85937-331-3	£17.99
Bradford (pb)	1-85937-204-x	£9.99	Essex - Second Selection	1-85937-456-5	£14.99
Bridgend (pb)	1-85937-386-0	£7.99	Essex (pb)	1-85937-270-8	£9.99
Bridgwater (pb)	1-85937-305-4	£9.99	Essex Coast	1-85937-342-9	£14.99
Bridport (pb)	1-85937-327-5	£9.99	Essex Living Memories	1-85937-490-5	£14.99
Brighton (pb)	1-85937-192-2	£8.99	Exeter	1-85937-539-1	£9.99
Bristol (pb)	1-85937-264-3	£9.99	Exmoor (pb)	1-85937-608-8	£9.99
British Life A Century Ago (pb)	1-85937-213-9	£9.99	Falmouth (pb)	1-85937-594-4	£9.99
Buckinghamshire (pb)	1-85937-200-7	£9.99	Folkestone (pb)	1-85937-124-8	£9.99
Camberley (pb)	1-85937-222-8	£9.99	Frome (pb)	1-85937-317-8	£9.99
Cambridge (pb)	1-85937-422-0	£9.99	Glamorgan	1-85937-488-3	£14.99
Cambridgeshire (pb)	1-85937-420-4	£9.99	Glasgow (pb)	1-85937-190-6	£9.99
Cambridgeshire Villages	1-85937-523-5	£14.99	Glastonbury (pb)	1-85937-338-0	£7.99
Canals And Waterways (pb)	1-85937-291-0	£9.99	Gloucester (pb)	1-85937-232-5	£9.99
Canterbury Cathedral (pb)	1-85937-179-5	£9.99	Gloucestershire (pb)	1-85937-561-8	£9.99
Cardiff (pb)	1-85937-093-4	£9.99	Great Yarmouth (pb)	1-85937-426-3	£9.99
Carmarthenshire (pb)	1-85937-604-5	£9.99	Greater Manchester (pb)	1-85937-266-x	£9.99
Chelmsford (pb)	1-85937-310-0	£9.99	Guildford (pb)	1-85937-410-7	£9.99
Cheltenham (pb)	1-85937-095-0	£9.99	Hampshire (pb)	1-85937-279-1	£9.99
Cheshire (pb)	1-85937-271-6	£9.99	Harrogate (pb)	1-85937-423-9	£9.99
Chester (pb)	1-85937-382 8	£9.99	Hastings and Bexhill (pb)	1-85937-131-0	£9.99
Chesterfield (pb)	1-85937-378-x	£9.99	Heart of Lancashire (pb)	1-85937-197-3	£9.99
Chichester (pb)	1-85937-228-7	£9.99	Helston (pb)	1-85937-214-7	£9.99
Churches of East Cornwall (pb)	1-85937-249-x	£9.99	Hereford (pb)	1-85937-175-2	£9.99
Churches of Hampshire (pb)	1-85937-207-4	£9.99	Herefordshire (pb)	1-85937-567-7	£9.99
Cinque Ports & Two Ancient Towns	1-85937-492-1	£14.99	Herefordshire Living Memories	1-85937-514-6	£14.99
Colchester (pb)	1-85937-188-4	£8.99	Hertfordshire (pb)	1-85937-247-3	£9.99
Cornwall (pb)	1-85937-229-5	£9.99	Horsham (pb)	1-85937-432-8	£9.99
Cornwall Living Memories	1-85937-248-1	£14.99	Humberside (pb)	1-85937-605-3	£9.99
Cotswolds (pb)	1-85937-230-9	£9.99	Hythe, Romney Marsh, Ashford (pb)	1-85937-256-2	£9.99
Cotswolds Living Memories	1-85937-255-4	£14.99	Ipswich (pb)	1-85937-424-7	£9.99
County Durham (pb)	1-85937-398-4	£9.99	Isle of Man (pb)	1-85937-268-6	£9.99
Croydon Living Memories (pb)	1-85937-162-0	£9.99	Isle of Wight (pb)	1-85937-429-8	£9.99
Cumbria (pb)	1-85937-621-5	£9.99	Isle of Wight Living Memories	1-85937-304-6	£14.99
Derby (pb)	1-85937-367-4	£9.99	Kent (pb)	1-85937-189-2	£9.99
Derbyshire (pb)	1-85937-196-5	£9.99	Kent Living Memories(pb)	1-85937-401-8	£9.99
Derbyshire Living Memories	1-85937-330-5	£14.99	Kings Lynn (pb)	1-85937-334-8	£9.99

Available from your local bookshop or from the publisher

Frith Book Co Titles (continued)

Title	ISBN	Price	Title	ISBN	Price
Lake District (pb)	1-85937-275-9	£9.99	Sherborne (pb)	1-85937-301-1	£9.99
Lancashire Living Memories	1-85937-335-6	£14.99	Shrewsbury (pb)	1-85937-325-9	£9.99
Lancaster, Morecambe, Heysham (pb)	1-85937-233-3	£9.99	Shropshire (pb)	1-85937-326-7	£9.99
Leeds (pb)	1-85937-202-3	£9.99	Shropshire Living Memories	1-85937-643-6	£14.99
Leicester (pb)	1-85937-381-x	£9.99	Somerset	1-85937-153-1	£14.99
Leicestershire & Rutland Living Memories	1-85937-500-6	£12.99	South Devon Coast	1-85937-107-8	£14.99
Leicestershire (pb)	1-85937-185-x	£9.99	South Devon Living Memories (pb)	1-85937-609-6	£9.99
Lighthouses	1-85937-257-0	£9.99	South East London (pb)	1-85937-263-5	£9.99
Lincoln (pb)	1-85937-380-1	£9.99	South Somerset	1-85937-318-6	£14.99
Lincolnshire (pb)	1-85937-433-6	£9.99	South Wales	1-85937-519-7	£14.99
Liverpool and Merseyside (pb)	1-85937-234-1	£9.99	Southampton (pb)	1-85937-427-1	£9.99
London (pb)	1-85937-183-3	£9.99	Southend (pb)	1-85937-313-5	£9.99
London Living Memories	1-85937-454-9	£14.99	Southport (pb)	1-85937-425-5	£9.99
Ludlow (pb)	1-85937-176-0	£9.99	St Albans (pb)	1-85937-341-0	£9.99
Luton (pb)	1-85937-235-x	£9.99	St Ives (pb)	1-85937-415-8	£9.99
Maidenhead (pb)	1-85937-339-9	£9.99	Stafford Living Memories (pb)	1-85937-503-0	£9.99
Maidstone (pb)	1-85937-391-7	£9.99	Staffordshire (pb)	1-85937-308-9	£9.99
Manchester (pb)	1-85937-198-1	£9.99	Stourbridge (pb)	1-85937-530-8	£9.99
Marlborough (pb)	1-85937-336-4	£9.99	Stratford upon Avon (pb)	1-85937-388-7	£9.99
Middlesex	1-85937-158-2	£14.99	Suffolk (pb)	1-85937-221-x	£9.99
Monmouthshire	1-85937-532-4	£14.99	Suffolk Coast (pb)	1-85937-610-x	£9.99
New Forest (pb)	1-85937-390-9	£9.99	Surrey (pb)	1-85937-240-6	£9.99
Newark (pb)	1-85937-366-6	£9.99	Surrey Living Memories	1-85937-328-3	£14.99
Newport, Wales (pb)	1-85937-258-9	£9.99	Sussex (pb)	1-85937-184-1	£9.99
Newquay (pb)	1-85937-421-2	£9.99	Sutton (pb)	1-85937-337-2	£9.99
Norfolk (pb)	1-85937-195-7	£9.99	Swansea (pb)	1-85937-167-1	£9.99
Norfolk Broads	1-85937-486-7	£14.99	Taunton (pb)	1-85937-314-3	£9.99
Norfolk Living Memories (pb)	1-85937-402-6	£9.99	Tees Valley & Cleveland (pb)	1-85937-623-1	£9.99
North Buckinghamshire	1-85937-626-6	£14.99	Teignmouth (pb)	1-85937-370-4	£7.99
North Devon Living Memories	1-85937-261-9	£14.99	Thanet (pb)	1-85937-116-7	£9.99
North Hertfordshire	1-85937-547-2	£14.99	Tiverton (pb)	1-85937-178-7	£9.99
North London (pb)	1-85937-403-4	£9.99	Torbay (pb)	1-85937-597-9	£9.99
North Somerset	1-85937-302-x	£14.99	Truro (pb)	1-85937-598-7	£9.99
North Wales (pb)	1-85937-298-8	£9.99	Victorian & Edwardian Dorset	1-85937-254-6	£14.99
North Yorkshire (pb)	1-85937-236-8	£9.99	Victorian & Edwardian Kent (pb)	1-85937-624-X	£9.99
Northamptonshire Living Memories	1-85937-529-4	£14.99	Victorian & Edwardian Maritime Album (pb)	1-85937-622-3	£9.99
Northamptonshire	1-85937-150-7	£14.99	Victorian and Edwardian Sussex (pb)	1-85937-625-8	£9.99
Northumberland Tyne & Wear (pb)	1-85937-281-3	£9.99	Villages of Devon (pb)	1-85937-293-7	£9.99
Northumberland	1-85937-522-7	£14.99	Villages of Kent (pb)	1-85937-294-5	£9.99
Norwich (pb)	1-85937-194-9	£8.99	Villages of Sussex (pb)	1-85937-295-3	£9.99
Nottingham (pb)	1-85937-324-0	£9.99	Warrington (pb)	1-85937-507-3	£9.99
Nottinghamshire (pb)	1-85937-187-6	£9.99	Warwick (pb)	1-85937-518-9	£9.99
Oxford (pb)	1-85937-411-5	£9.99	Warwickshire (pb)	1-85937-203-1	£9.99
Oxfordshire (pb)	1-85937-430-1	£9.99	Welsh Castles (pb)	1-85937-322-4	£9.99
Oxfordshire Living Memories	1-85937-525-1	£14.99	West Midlands (pb)	1-85937-289-9	£9.99
Paignton (pb)	1-85937-374-7	£7.99	West Sussex (pb)	1-85937-607-x	£9.99
Peak District (pb)	1-85937-280-5	£9.99	West Yorkshire (pb)	1-85937-201-5	£9.99
Pembrokeshire	1-85937-262-7	£14.99	Weston Super Mare (pb)	1-85937-306-2	£9.99
Penzance (pb)	1-85937-595-2	£9.99	Weymouth (pb)	1-85937-209-0	£9.99
Peterborough (pb)	1-85937-219-8	£9.99	Wiltshire (pb)	1-85937-277-5	£9.99
Picturesque Harbours	1-85937-208-2	£14.99	Wiltshire Churches (pb)	1-85937-171-x	£9.99
Piers	1-85937-237-6	£17.99	Wiltshire Living Memories (pb)	1-85937-396-8	£9.99
Plymouth (pb)	1-85937-389-5	£9.99	Winchester (pb)	1-85937-428-x	£9.99
Poole & Sandbanks (pb)	1-85937-251-1	£9.99	Windsor (pb)	1-85937-333-x	£9.99
Preston (pb)	1-85937-212-0	£9.99	Wokingham & Bracknell (pb)	1-85937-329-1	£9.99
Reading (pb)	1-85937-238-4	£9.99	Woodbridge (pb)	1-85937-498-0	£9.99
Redhill to Reigate (pb)	1-85937-596-0	£9.99	Worcester (pb)	1-85937-165-5	£9.99
Ringwood (pb)	1-85937-384-4	£7.99	Worcestershire Living Memories	1-85937-489-1	£14.99
Romford (pb)	1-85937-319-4	£9.99	Worcestershire	1-85937-152-3	£14.99
Royal Tunbridge Wells (pb)	1-85937-504-9	£9.99	York (pb)	1-85937-199-x	£9.99
Salisbury (pb)	1-85937-239-2	£9.99	Yorkshire (pb)	1-85937-186-8	£9.99
Scarborough (pb)	1-85937-379-8	£9.99	Yorkshire Coastal Memories	1-85937-506-5	£14.99
Sevenoaks and Tonbridge (pb)	1-85937-392-5	£9.99	Yorkshire Dales	1-85937-502-2	£14.99
Sheffield & South Yorks (pb)	1-85937-267-8	£9.99	Yorkshire Living Memories (pb)	1-85937-397-6	£9.99

See Frith books on the internet at www.francisfrith.co.uk

FRITH PRODUCTS & SERVICES

Francis Frith would doubtless be pleased to know that the pioneering publishing venture he started in 1860 still continues today. Over a hundred and forty years later, The Francis Frith Collection continues in the same innovative tradition and is now one of the foremost publishers of vintage photographs in the world. Some of the current activities include:

Interior Decoration

Today Frith's photographs can be seen framed and as giant wall murals in thousands of pubs, restaurants, hotels, banks, retail stores and other public buildings throughout the country. In every case they enhance the unique local atmosphere of the places they depict and provide reminders of gentler days in an increasingly busy and frenetic world.

Product Promotions

Frith products are used by many major companies to promote the sales of their own products or to reinforce their own history and heritage. Frith promotions have been used by Hovis bread, Courage beers, Scots Porage Oats, Colman's mustard, Cadbury's foods, Mellow Birds coffee, Dunhill pipe tobacco, Guinness, and Bulmer's Cider.

Genealogy and Family History

As the interest in family history and roots grows world-wide, more and more people are turning to Frith's photographs of Great Britain for images of the towns, villages and streets where their ancestors lived; and, of course, photographs of the churches and chapels where their ancestors were christened, married and buried are an essential part of every genealogy tree and family album.

Frith Products

All Frith photographs are available Framed or just as Mounted Prints and Posters (size 23 x 16 inches). These may be ordered from the address below. From time to time other products - Address Books, Calendars, Table Mats, etc - are available.

The Internet

Already fifty thousand Frith photographs can be viewed and purchased on the internet through the Frith websites and a myriad of partner sites.

For more detailed information on Frith companies and products, look at these sites:

www.francisfrith.co.uk
www.francisfrith.com
(for North American visitors)

See the complete list of Frith Books at:

www.francisfrith.co.uk

This web site is regularly updated with the latest list of publications from the Frith Book Company. If you wish to buy books relating to another part of the country that your local bookshop does not stock, you may purchase on-line.

For further information, trade, or author enquiries please contact us at the address below:
The Francis Frith Collection, Frith's Barn, Teffont, Salisbury, Wiltshire, England SP3 5QP.
Tel: +44 (0)1722 716 376 Fax: +44 (0)1722 716 881 Email: sales@francisfrith.co.uk

See Frith books on the internet at www.francisfrith.co.uk

FREE PRINT OF YOUR CHOICE

Mounted Print
Overall size 14 x 11 inches (355 x 280mm)

Choose any Frith photograph in this book.
Simply complete the Voucher opposite and return it with your remittance for £2.25 (to cover postage and handling) and we will print the photograph of your choice in SEPIA (size 11 x 8 inches) and supply it in a cream mount with a burgundy rule line (overall size 14 x 11 inches).
Please note: photographs with a reference number starting with a "Z" are not Frith photographs and cannot be supplied under this offer.
Offer valid for delivery to UK addresses only.

PLUS: Order additional Mounted Prints at HALF PRICE - £7.49 each (normally £14.99)
If you would like to order more Frith prints from this book, possibly as gifts for friends and family, you can buy them at half price (with no additional postage and handling costs).

PLUS: Have your Mounted Prints framed
For an extra £14.95 per print you can have your mounted print(s) framed in an elegant polished wood and gilt moulding, overall size 16 x 13 inches (no additional postage and handling required).

IMPORTANT!

These special prices are only available if you use this form to order. You must use the ORIGINAL VOUCHER on this page (no copies permitted). We can only despatch to one address. This offer cannot be combined with any other offer.

Send completed Voucher form to:
The Francis Frith Collection, Frith's Barn, Teffont, Salisbury, Wiltshire SP3 5QP

CHOOSE A PHOTOGRAPH FROM THIS BOOK

Voucher for **FREE** and Reduced Price *Frith Prints*

Please do not photocopy this voucher. Only the original is valid, so please fill it in, cut it out and return it to us with your order.

Picture ref no	Page no	Qty	Mounted @ £7.49	Framed + £14.95	Total Cost
		1	Free of charge*	£	£
			£7.49	£	£
			£7.49	£	£
			£7.49	£	£
			£7.49	£	£
			£7.49	£	£

Please allow 28 days for delivery

* Post & handling (UK)	£2.25
Total Order Cost	£

Title of this book . . . .

I enclose a cheque/postal order for £ . . . .
made payable to 'The Francis Frith Collection'

OR please debit my Mastercard / Visa / Switch (Maestro) /Amex card
(credit cards please on all overseas orders), details below

Card Number

Issue No (Switch only)   Valid from (Amex/Switch)

Expires   Signature

Name Mr/Mrs/Ms . . . .

Address . . . .
. . . .
. . . .
. . . . Postcode . . . .

Daytime Tel No . . . .

Email . . . .

Valid to 31/12/07

Would you like to find out more about Francis Frith?

We have recently recruited some entertaining speakers who are happy to visit local groups, clubs and societies to give an illustrated talk documenting Frith's travels and photographs. If you are a member of such a group and are interested in hosting a presentation, we would love to hear from you.

Our speakers bring with them a small selection of our local town and county books, together with sample prints. They are happy to take orders. A small proportion of the order value is donated to the group who have hosted the presentation. The talks are therefore an excellent way of fundraising for small groups and societies.

Can you help us with information about any of the Frith photographs in this book?

We are gradually compiling an historical record for each of the photographs in the Frith archive. It is always fascinating to find out the names of the people shown in the pictures, as well as insights into the shops, buildings and other features depicted.

If you recognize anyone in the photographs in this book, or if you have information not already included in the author's caption, do let us know. We would love to hear from you, and will try to publish it in future books or articles.

Our production team

Frith books are produced by a small dedicated team at offices in the converted Grade II listed 18th-century barn at Teffont near Salisbury, illustrated above. Most have worked with the Frith Collection for many years. All have in common one quality: they have a passion for the Frith Collection. The team is constantly expanding, but currently includes:

Paul Baron, Phillip Brennan, Jason Buck, John Buck, Ruth Butler, Heather Crisp, David Davies, Louis du Mont, Isobel Hall, Gareth Harris, Lucy Hart, Julian Hight, Peter Horne, James Kinnear, Karen Kinnear, Tina Leary, Stuart Login, David Marsh, Lesley-Ann Millard, Sue Molloy, Glenda Morgan, Wayne Morgan, Sarah Roberts, Kate Rotondetto, Dean Scource, Eliza Sackett, Terence Sackett, Sandra Sampson, Adrian Sanders, Sandra Sanger, Jan Scrivens, Julia Skinner, David Smith, Miles Smith, Lewis Taylor, Shelley Tolcher, Lorraine Tuck, Amanita Wainwright and Ricky Williams.

Free Print - see overleaf